Remembering
Knoxville

William E. Hardy

TURNER
PUBLISHING COMPANY

In 1865, James Spears Hall, who resided in the Halls community, founded J. S. Hall, a retail clothing store located at 16 Market Street. After Hall's death in 1906, his sons, William and James, continued the successful family business, which manufactured suits, shoes, and hats for men. Later the firm expanded its line to include clothing for women and opened new stores at both 318-320 Gay Street and in the Western Plaza on Kingston Pike. The business is shown here around the 1890s.

Remembering
Knoxville

Turner Publishing Company
www.turnerpublishing.com

Remembering Knoxville

Copyright © 2010 Turner Publishing Company

Library of Congress Control Number: 2010924249

ISBN: 978-1-59652-639-6

Printed in the United States of America

ISBN: 978-1-68336-845-8 (pbk.)

Contents

This wintry scene of the Gay Street Bridge and Knoxville taken from the south shore of the Tennessee River captures an unusual sight: one of the rare moments in the city's history when the river was frozen solid (ca. 1910s).

ACKNOWLEDGMENTS

This volume, *Remembering Knoxville,* is the result of the cooperation and efforts of many individuals, organizations, and corporations. It is with great thanks that we acknowledge the valuable contribution of the following for their generous support:

Library of Congress
McClung Collection
Tennessee State Library
Thompson Collection
University of Tennessee Knoxville

We would also like to thank the following individuals for valuable contributions and assistance in making this work possible:

Nick Wyman, William B. Eigelsbach, Elizabeth Dunham (Special Collections, University of Tennessee, Knoxville)

PREFACE

Knoxville has thousands of historic photographs that reside in archives, both locally and nationally. This book began with the observation that, while those photographs are of great interest to many, they are not easily accessible. During a time when Knoxville is looking ahead and evaluating its future course, many people are asking, How do we treat the past? These decisions affect every aspect of the city—architecture, public spaces, commerce, infrastructure—and these, in turn, affect the way that people live their lives. This book seeks to provide easy access to a valuable, objective look into the history of Knoxville.

The power of photographs is that they are less subjective than words in their treatment of history. Although the photographer can make subjective decisions regarding subject matter and how to capture and present it, photographs seldom interpret the past to the extent textual histories can. For this reason, photography is uniquely positioned to offer an original, untainted look at the past, allowing the viewer to learn for himself what the world was like a century or more ago.

This project represents countless hours of review and research. The researchers and writer have reviewed thousands of photographs in numerous archives. We greatly appreciate the generous assistance of those listed in the acknowledgments of this work, without whom this project could not have been completed.

The goal in publishing this work is to provide broader access to this set of extraordinary photographs that seek to inspire, provide perspective, and evoke insight that might assist people who are responsible for determining Knoxville's future. In addition, the book seeks to preserve the past with adequate respect and reverence.

With the exception of touching up imperfections that have accrued with the passage of time and cropping where necessary, no changes have been made. The focus and clarity of many images are limited to the technology and the ability of the photographer at the time they were recorded.

The work is divided into eras. Beginning with some of the earliest known photographs of Knoxville, the first section records photographs through the end of the nineteenth century. The second section spans the beginning of the twentieth century through World War I. Section Three moves to the era between the wars, and the last section covers the 1940s to recent times.

In each of these sections we have made an effort to capture various aspects of life through our selection of photographs. People, commerce, transportation, infrastructure, religious institutions, and educational institutions have been included to provide a broad perspective.

We encourage readers to reflect as they go walking in Knoxville, strolling through the city, its parks, and its neighborhoods. It is the publisher's hope that in utilizing this work, longtime residents will learn something new and that new residents will gain a perspective on where Knoxville has been, so that each can contribute to its future.

—*Todd Bottorff, Publisher*

A coal conveyor in one of the Myers-Whaley mines loads coal into a cart. Knoxville, strategically located in the center of a coal-producing region, was the headquarters of several coal-mining companies at the turn of the century.

FROM THE CIVIL WAR TO THE CENTENNIAL

(1859–1899)

Union soldiers encamp on the grounds of the Tennessee Deaf and Dumb Asylum located on Asylum Street (present-day Summitt Hill) in 1864. Ground was broken in 1848 and the school opened in 1851. The school closed during the Civil War as Confederate and Union armies began using the building as a military hospital. The building served as a school until 1924 when it became City Hall.

The environs of Knoxville as viewed from the south bank of the Holston River during the Civil War. (An 1890 federal statute recognized the junction of the French Broad and Holston rivers, to the east of Knoxville, as the root of the Tennessee River.) Union encampments at Fort Stanley appear in the foreground, and the three buildings that constituted East Tennessee University can be observed atop Barbara Hill across the river (1864).

The Strawberry Plains Bridge across the Holston River was one of several bridges targeted in November 1861 by the bridge burners, a group of East Tennessee Unionists. However, a lone Confederate sentry was able to fend off 13 Unionists sent to burn the bridge. The group lost their matches and nerves when the Rebel soldier fired, wounding two men. During the course of the Civil War, the bridge was destroyed and rebuilt four times (1864).

Colonel Orville Babcock, seated on a tree stump, and Captain Orlando Poe pose for a photograph inside Fort Sanders in 1864. The fort, a hastily built yet bastioned Union earthwork, located west of Knoxville, was the scene of an ill-conceived Confederate frontal assault that resulted in the massacre of troops that the Confederacy could not afford to lose. The Confederates' failure to capture Knoxville guaranteed Union control over the city and the majority of East Tennessee.

Gay Street has always been Knoxville's principal thoroughfare. This 1869 photograph captures Knoxville's thriving business district along Gay Street four years after the Civil War nearly destroyed the city. Businesses along Gay included a real estate company, stores selling shoes and hats and jewelry, at least two drugstores, two hardware stores, two bookstores, T. M. Schleier's Picture Gallery, and a "Messenger of Peace."

Railroad bridges, such as this one at Platt Creek near Knoxville, were targets for both Confederate and Union armies. The railroad in East Tennessee was critical to the Confederacy because it served as a direct link between Richmond and the Deep South. But with Union forces approaching Confederate armies in East Tennessee during the fall of 1863, the Confederacy destroyed railroad bridges to slow the Union advance (1864).

Knoxville lay in ruins following the 1863 Siege of Knoxville. This view faces southward toward both the military bridge at Strawberry Plains and one of several defensive earthworks in and around the vicinity of Knoxville (1864).

On September 21, 1877, President Rutherford B. Hayes became the second sitting president of the United States to visit Knoxville (the first was Andrew Jackson in 1830). Knoxvillians turned out in large numbers to welcome the president in a ceremony conducted in front of the Lamar House. Following the ceremony, Hayes departed for Atlanta but returned on September 23 and attended church services at First Methodist Church.

The Gay Street Bridge as it appeared in 1880 from the south bank of the Tennessee River. The bridge was rebuilt twice following the Civil War when an 1867 flood swept the first bridge away and a tornado destroyed the second bridge in 1875. Because of the instability of the bridge, local officials enforced the city's first speed limit and imposed a five-dollar fine for passengers who crossed over the river faster than a walk.

This photograph captures the crowds that gathered to witness the first train from Louisville, Kentucky, to Knoxville, which arrived June 3, 1883. Although completing the direct route took many years, Knoxvillians celebrated the historic moment that linked their city with the Midwest.

As of the end of the Civil War, Knoxville still lacked a regular police force. A spike in robberies in the late 1860s led city officials to appoint a secret police force. By the early 1880s, the board of mayor and aldermen had instituted Knoxville's first professional police force. This photograph, taken in front of City Hall in 1883, indicates not only an expanding police force but also an integrated department with two black officers.

Looking across Cumberland Avenue from the current site of the World's Fair Park toward Old College on "the Hill" at the University of Tennessee. During the Civil War, Confederate and Union forces occupied the campus, then known as East Tennessee University, using the school's buildings as military hospitals. The school reopened after the war at the nearby Tennessee Deaf and Dumb Asylum until the campus and its buildings could be repaired.

The University of Tennessee's 1893 baseball team poses for their photograph. Until the 1910s, the university's baseball team attracted more spectators than the football team did. Nearly 250 persons accompanied the UT baseball team as they traveled to play local rivals such as Maryville and Vanderbilt.

Knoxville's earliest houses were log cabins. These three men pose for a photograph in front of a two-story log structure.

Second Presbyterian Church formed in 1818 when an internal struggle in the First Presbyterian Church congregation divided their numbers. The church was originally located on Clinch Avenue at the northeast corner of Market until moving to this location in 1906 at the intersection of Church and Walnut streets. In 1957, the congregation moved into their present building, which is located on Kingston Pike in West Knoxville.

Knoxville's board of mayor and aldermen established the Knoxville Fire Company in 1822. According to city laws, males between the ages of 15 and 50 were required to serve in the company, and all establishments including dwellings were expected to own a bucket that could hold at least two gallons of water. On March 17, 1885, the City of Knoxville formed its first fully professional paid fire department, hiring 15 firemen (ca. 1890).

This photograph reveals the ruins left by the devastating inferno of April 8, 1897, which destroyed an entire city block.

A bird's-eye view of Knoxville's skyline facing south toward the Tennessee River and the Great Smoky Mountains.

Looking south on Clinch Avenue from the western side of Market House known as "watermelon row." Farmers and ranchers who could not afford the price to rent a stall inside the Market House were allowed to set up their wagons outside to sell their products. Watermelon row became a popular location for many Knoxvillians because products could often be purchased for less money than those found inside the Market House.

Members of the Knoxville Fire Department pose in front of their headquarters located at the north end of Market Square. Following the great fire of 1897, dubbed the "Million Dollar Fire," the city's board of mayor and aldermen worked to secure monies to augment the department's budget to acquire new equipment and additional personnel (1897).

Dust kicked up along Gay Street was a constant nuisance for Knoxville's citizens as they visited the city's business district to shop for goods. This young boy sprinkled water in front of stores along the downtown thoroughfare to keep the dust settled.

Hope Brothers Jewelry Store was located "at the clock," a famous landmark at 142 Gay Street. In this photograph, the base of the clock with the "Hope" logo is visible to the right of the young boy. In 1868, David James Hope and John W. Hope reorganized their father's business and began selling watches and jewelry.

Streetcar service was introduced to Knoxville in 1876. With the advent of electricity to the city in 1885, the idea of converting streetcars to electric power was not far behind. On May 1, 1890, the first electric streetcar debuted, seen here on a line running out of Magnolia Avenue to Lake Ottosee (now Chilhowee Park). Soon thereafter, all lines were converted to electric power.

Turn of the Century and Beyond

(1900–1919)

Couriers with the Knoxville-Sevierville Fast Mail Service pose in front of Thurman and Loveday (ca. 1910).

Spanish-American War soldiers parade triumphantly down Gay Street.

A train pulls into the Southern Railway Station. The railroad was the key to Knoxville's postwar economic growth. Because of its geographical location, Knoxville served as a commercial hub for the Appalachian South. Goods arriving in the city from the Northeast and Midwest were distributed throughout the region.

The Atkin Hotel, at the corner of Gay and Depot, was conveniently located to serve the traveling public arriving by train at the Southern Depot across the street. The Atkin advertised 200 fireproof rooms, 150 of which included a bath.

The Imperial Hotel stands at the corner of Gay and Clinch in the early 1900s. The hotel was a popular home away from home until a fire destroyed the building in 1916. The following year, a triumvirate of financiers known as the "Three Musketeers" or the "One Hundred Per Cent Club," which included William Cary Ross, Benjamin Andrew Morton, and Hugh Wheeler Sanford, pooled their capital to replace the Imperial with the completely fireproof Farragut Hotel.

The circus arrives in Knoxville in the early twentieth century as onlookers gaze at the exotic sight of elephants marching down Gay Street. During the "Golden Age" of the American circus in this era, performers and animals often paraded through the streets of a city in full costume to alert locals that the circus was in town.

This photograph captures the efficiency of Knoxville's Fire Department. Firemen atop a horse-drawn hook and ladder truck prepare for action as they pass the Southern Railway Depot. In the wake of the terrible "Million Dollar Fire," this image may have been staged to resolve fears among citizens about the fire department's ability to respond quickly (ca. 1905).

Located a few miles north of Knoxville, Fountain City began to boom in 1890 when a steam railway began operating between both cities. F. G. Phillips was hired to design a heart-shaped lake with a walkway surrounded by white picket fences. Knoxville's most prominent families built summer homes that overlooked the park and lake, the point that marked the end of the street railway line. In 1962, Fountain City was annexed to Knoxville (ca. 1900).

Indicative of the region's strong Unionist sentiment during the Civil War, this large Gothic Revival–style monument stands on the grounds of the Knoxville National Cemetery. Erected between 1890 and 1901, this memorial to the Union, known locally as the Tennessee or Wilder monument, is the largest Union monument in the South (ca. 1906).

The U.S. Post Office and Custom House, erected in 1874 at the corner of Clinch and Market, was Knoxville's first federal building. Designed by Alfred B. Mullett, the building was constructed in the neoclassical Italianate style with East Tennessee marble. The original building has been expanded twice, in 1910 and 2004. Today, the building is home to the East Tennessee Historical Society, the Calvin M. McClung Historical Collection, and the Knox County Archives.

After countless delays and built at a cost far exceeding the original bid, Science Hall, located on the southeastern rim of "the Hill," opened on March 3, 1892, as Professor T. C. Karns spoke on the subject "Old Times at the University" to an estimated crowd of 700 persons. The building had steam heating. A new dynamo and a 40 horsepower engine were installed to furnish electricity for the structure (ca. 1903).

A 1903 view of "the Hill" at the University of Tennessee from the south bank of the Tennessee River. Many years would pass before the campus expanded much. At the turn of the century, the university's enrollment peaked at approximately 750, a statistic dwarfed by the nearly 26,500 students enrolled in 2007.

The Cumberland Club owned this building located at the corner of Walnut Street and Clinch. The club met for the sole purpose of its members' social enjoyment. The Cumberland Club was accused in June 1915 of keeping liquor on the premises, defined as a misdemeanor by Knoxville law of the time (ca. 1905).

The Episcopal congregation struggled for nearly 20 years to establish a foothold in Knoxville. On May 9, 1844, St. John's Episcopal Church and its group of 25 communicants became the first mission of the Episcopal faith to open in the eastern part of Tennessee. The original church was razed in 1891 and replaced with this much larger facility on the same corner at Cumberland and Walnut (ca. 1903).

A view of Gay Street, facing north from Clinch Avenue in the early 1900s.

Inspired by expositions held in numerous American cities in the 1890s and early 1900s, several prominent local businessmen belonging to the Knoxville Commercial Club managed to bring the Appalachian Exposition to the city in 1910. Held in Chilhowee Park from September 12 to October 12, the exposition attracted hundreds of thousands of visitors. The Central Administrative Building (later changed to the Machinery and Liberal Arts Building) pictured here contained 80,000 square feet of exhibit space.

Patrons gather at the main entrance to Chilhowee Park to purchase tickets before entering the 1910 Appalachian Exposition. The wings above the arch hold a large medallion and the letters "AE," the symbol of the exposition. Knoxville's boosters, who were responsible for bringing the exposition to the city, sought to promote the modernization of their region by bringing the natural resources of southern Appalachia to the attention of American businessmen.

42

Patrons to the 1913 National Conservation Exposition approach the Land Building in the background. The Land Building was the exposition's second-largest structure, housing exhibits that focused on water and forest resources, soil, fossil fuels, and wildlife. A playground to entertain children was located next to the Land Building.

During the 1913 National Conservation Exposition, the Negro Building contained numerous exhibits focusing on the life and work of African-Americans.

A bear den at Chilhowee Park, located a few miles east of Knoxville.

Looking south on Market Street from Union Avenue, early automobiles line the street.

There were no modern-day grocery stores in Knoxville before 1930. This early-twentieth-century photograph captures the interior of G. R. Hurst's grocery market located at 1845 Euclid Avenue.

Vendors line up along the eastern side of the Market House to sell produce from their wagons and trucks. This popular section of the Market House was often very congested, prompting city officials to impose a five-dollar fine on those who, if they could manage to do so, drove faster than a walk through the busy side street.

In this view facing north from the 500 block of Gay Street at Union Avenue, banners festoon the city's main thoroughfare advertising J. S. Hall's Clothing Company and Nathan Kuhlman's drugstores. This form of advertising was used frequently in the early decades of the twentieth century (ca. 1910).

In 1885, the Knox County government moved across the street from its original quarters into a new courthouse pictured here, which was located on the south side of Main at the corner of Gay.

In 1894, Nathan Kuhlman opened his drugstore at 301 Gay Street. Thirteen years later, he was operating three drugstores in the city. An astute businessman, Kuhlman festooned several banners across Gay and other city streets to attract the attention of shoppers. In this photograph taken at the turn of the twentieth century, Kuhlman's store number 2 advertises 7 cigars for the bargain price of 25 cents.

This December 1910 photograph, taken during the noon hour, shows some of the young boys and a girl who worked half-days at Brookside Cotton Mills. Founded in 1885, Brookside was the largest textile mill in Knoxville, employing 1,200 workers. In the early twentieth century, there were more people with manufacturing and mechanical jobs than were engaged in commerce. Textile and apparel manufacturing continued to grow in Knoxville, peaking in the 1920s.

The telegraph was slow in coming to Knoxville, having reached the city sometime between 1858 and 1859. The Postal Telegraph Company, for whom these young unidentified telegraph boys are working, entered Knoxville in 1900. The company was absorbed during World War II by Western Union.

Two young employees of Knoxville Knitting Mills leave work around 1910.

Between the World Wars

(1920–1939)

Lake Ottosee located in Chilhowee Park was a favorite spot for family gatherings and company picnics complete with food, games, music, and fireworks. The park became a popular leisure spot in the wake of the Appalachian and National Conservation expositions. The lake was available not only for boating but also for swimming. These Knoxvillians enjoy cooling off on a warm summer afternoon.

Ayres Hall, a Gothic building of brick and cast stone with a clock tower and three-story wings, is the symbol of the University of Tennessee, Knoxville. Named in honor of Dr. Brown Ayres, who served as the university's president from 1904 to 1919, Ayres Hall was completed in 1921 at a cost of $300,000.

Famed Union Civil War admiral David G. Farragut was born in this cabin at Campbell's Station, which was located several miles west of Knoxville and is today a burgeoning suburb named in honor of Farragut, the Battle of Mobile Bay hero. The pioneer log cabin was dismantled and reassembled in Chilhowee Park for the Appalachian Exposition. It was later destroyed by fire.

This mill wheel and housing was built to serve as the entrance gate into the Westmoreland Heights community, which is located in West Knoxville at Westland and Sherwood Drive.

Located in North Knoxville at 211 West Fifth Avenue, the First Christian Church's congregation began worshiping in this building in 1915 after meeting at various locations throughout the city following the establishment of the church in 1874. The Christian Church (Disciples of Christ) was founded in the early 1800s in the United States, and today a large number of the church's nearly 4,000 congregations are in Tennessee.

An early University of Tennessee football game is under way on Wait Field. Between 1908 and 1921, the university's football team played their games on a field tightly bound by a few rows of wooden bleachers, a fence, and a steep embankment, with no room for expansion. The gridiron itself was hard on the players—gravel was constantly kicked up to scrape elbows and knees. Today the Walters Life Sciences Building occupies the site of Wait Field.

In view here are the ice-choked waters of the Tennessee River in 1917, a rare event.

Named in honor of Civil War admiral David G. Farragut, the Farragut Hotel opened on February 1, 1919, at the corner of Gay and Clinch. The Farragut was advertised as completely fireproof with a ceiling fan in every room. The Farragut's owners enjoyed ten years of unrivaled success until the Andrew Johnson Hotel opened a few blocks south on Gay Street and began to compete (ca. 1920).

This view of Gay Street looking north between Commerce and Vine depicts the terrain before the dip was filled in. In the distance, the iron bridge that crossed over the railroad tracks connected downtown to North Knoxville. Horses, streetcars, and automobiles competing for space made the bridge difficult to navigate. The last remaining tree on Gay Street, at left, was said to be more than 80 years old when it fell in November 1930.

Plans to replace Wait Field began in 1919 as money donated by W. S. Shields and his wife, Alice Watkins, along with matching university funds, enabled UT to build stands that could accommodate 3,200 spectators. The new Shields-Watkins Field, however, remained rough and uneven. To address the irregularities, UT's president canceled classes, declaring March 16, 1921, a "digging holiday." Equipped with picks, shovels, and wheelbarrows, students and faculty members labored to level the field.

This photograph captures the scene on the Upper Parade Ground shortly after a game with collegiate rival Vanderbilt. The Old Jefferson Hall, which appears in the background, and the Upper Parade Ground were located on the southern rim of "the Hill." These college men pose conspicuously—beneath equally conspicuous rooftop pitchers and benches . . .

Todd and Armistead drugstore is open for business at the intersection of Market and Clinch Street. Signage says suits can be pressed while you wait, Norris candies are exquisite, and parking is limited to one hour.

After a devastating 1928 fire, the Church Street Methodist Church debated whether to rebuild the church on Church Street or pick a different site. Preserving the church's name, the congregation decided to move to Henley Street, building a new structure there at a cost of $525,000. President Franklin Roosevelt reportedly remarked on his 1940 visit to Knoxville that the new structure was "the most beautiful church I have ever seen."

In 1926, Robert Foust, a creative dreamer, purchased 100 acres adjoining Sequoyah Hills, Knoxville's first planned subdivision. His vision for Talahi, which stems from the Cherokee phrase for "in the oaks," was to design a community surpassed in natural charm by no other location in America. Sequoyah Hills's posh houses, parks, sculptures, and fountains, such as the Panther Fountain shown here, have come to symbolize this exclusive Knoxville community.

Marble Springs Plantation, the home of Tennessee's first governor, John Sevier, is located at the foot of Bays Mountain, about five miles south of Knoxville. The land on which Marble Springs stands was originally a pioneer outpost when Sevier acquired the property from the State of North Carolina. While restoration efforts have reconstructed several of the plantation's buildings, the only original structure remaining is the main cabin.

The Southern Railway Depot, with its famed tower and weathervane, was erected at the north end of Gay Street at 318 West Depot Avenue in 1904. For nearly 70 years, the Southern Depot was a bustling point of entry to and departure from Knoxville, but competition from automobiles and airplanes led to the demise of passenger train service. On August 12, 1970, the city abandoned regularly scheduled passenger train service.

On January 15, 1843, a small group met and founded the First Baptist Church in the upper room of the Knox County Courthouse. As the church expanded, the congregation erected this structure in 1888 along Gay Street. To help finance construction, Knoxville entrepreneur W. W. Woodruff matched every dollar donated to the building fund by members. The First Baptist Church met here until moving in 1924 to its present location along Main Street.

In 1897, a new three-story block-long brick building was constructed on the site of the original Market House that had opened in 1854. Permanent stalls to be rented out by local vendors, who offered fresh meat, produce, and baked goods, were installed inside the building. The Market House stood until a fire started by a ten-year-old boy with a cigarette destroyed the building in 1960.

Before 1897, animals were butchered inside the Market House. Flies and blood-splattered stalls that had to be painted a dark red to hide the stains led officials to end the practice. Here a butcher sells beef at a numbered stall he is renting inside the market (ca. 1920).

Overlooking the horseshoe bend of the Tennessee River along Lyons View Drive a few miles west of downtown, the Cherokee Country Club pictured here was built in 1928 by Knoxville architects Joseph and Albert Baumann.

On the evening of June 29, 1938, a fire completely ravaged the Liberal Arts and Machinery Building located at Chilhowee Park, which had housed the exhibits that were displayed during the great expositions of the early 1910s. The building was later replaced with the Jacob Building, named in honor of Moses Jacob, who oversaw the East Tennessee Division Fair (Tennessee Valley Agricultural and Industrial Fair) from 1916 until his death in 1943.

Local farmers pulled their wagons and trucks up to the western side of the Market House to unload their goods for sale (ca. 1930).

Looking north on the western side of the Market House at the corner of Market Street and Union Avenue (ca. 1930).

Knoxville's first organized baseball franchise, the Indians, arrived in 1896 and took up residence at Baldwin Park, making official a lengthy baseball tradition in the Knoxville area that had begun in 1865 with a game between Unionists and Confederates. In 1931, the Mobile Bears, an A1 Southern Association team based in Mobile, Alabama, came to Knoxville and changed its name to the Smokies. The team played in Knoxville until returning to Mobile in 1944. In this 1934 photograph, the Smokies pose for a team portrait.

On March 8, 1909, the $50,000 Bijou Theatre opened at the corner of Gay and Cumberland. A packed house enjoyed George M. Cohan's "Little Johnny Jones," a popular Broadway musical. Even in the era of Jim Crow, the Bijou admitted blacks along with whites. Black patrons had to use a separate entrance and were relegated to a specific balcony.

The Tennessee Theatre, which opened on October 1, 1928, was built at an estimated cost of nearly $2,000,000. Patrons were charged 40 cents for matinees and 60 cents for evening shows. The theater was one of the first public places in Knoxville to install air-conditioning.

An automobile emerges from one of the numerous tunnels built during the Great Depression era in the Great Smoky Mountains National Park. President Franklin D. Roosevelt's New Deal programs used tax dollars to put a lot of unemployed Knoxvillians to work building roads, bridges, and tunnels.

Established in 1905, Draughon's Business College stood at the northeastern corner of Clinch Avenue and Market Street directly across from the U.S. Post Office and Custom House.

For the first half of the twentieth century, Miller's Department Store, located in the center of Knoxville's business district at the northwest corner of Gay Street and Union Avenue, was a pillar of the city's economy. But Miller's and other Knoxville department stores suffered following the construction of West Town Mall in West Knoxville in 1971. After nearly 70 years, Miller's closed in 1973 and the building was converted to office space.

Looking north on the eastern side of the Market House. For decades farmers lined the side of the Market House with first their wagons and later their trucks, laden with farm produce to sell to shoppers. T. E. Burns Company, a popular upscale grocery and bakery store, can be seen at the end of the block at the northeastern corner of Market and Wall.

Snow blankets the campus of the University of Tennessee. Barbara Blount Hall, the university's first women's dormitory, appears at left in this image.

John Housley Cigar Company was located in North Knoxville at 733-735 North Central Avenue near the intersection with Broadway. This photograph of Housley's storefront captures an advertising campaign for King Edward Cigars, a Swiss brand that used the likeness of King Edward VII to sell its products. After his ascension to the throne, King Edward proclaimed, "Gentlemen, you may smoke," thereby striking down Queen Victoria's ban on smoking.

This is an interior view of the United States Post Office, which was located on Main Avenue. Local architects Joseph and Albert Bauman designed this building constructed of assorted colors of Tennessee marble quarried in Knoxville. When the post office moved to this location in 1934, the Tennessee Valley Authority moved its headquarters to the Old Post Office and Custom House located on the corner of Clinch and Market.

Located at the southwestern corner of Gay and Clinch, the Tennessee Theatre is one of the few great movie palaces from the Roaring Twenties still in operation. On October 1, 1928, Knoxvillians purchased their 60-cent tickets to enter the $2,000,000 theater for the first time. Once inside, patrons gazed at the Spanish-Moorish style interior complete with a $50,000 Mighty Wurlitzer pipe organ that entertained them before the show.

The Henley Street Bridge spans the Tennessee River connecting the downtown area to South Knoxville. Construction on the Henley Street Bridge began in September 1931 and was completed in only 15 months during the midst of the Great Depression at a cost of about $1,000,000 to taxpayers. This photograph captures the amount of work completed by November 1, 1931.

S & W Cafeteria, a popular lunch and dinner destination for those who worked in Knoxville's downtown business district, was located along Gay Street between Clinch Avenue and Church Street next to the Tennessee Theatre. The two-story building had sufficient room to host large groups and organizations. An organ located on the first floor next to the staircase provided soothing music for diners.

George T. Fenton, president of Fenton Construction Company, which was located on Dale Avenue, owned this house atop a hill in West Knoxville along Kingston Pike.

In November 1921, WNAV became not only Knoxville's first radio station, but also one of the nation's first radio stations. Shortly thereafter, the station changed its call letters to WNOX. Originally located in the St. James Hotel on Wall Avenue, the station moved in 1935 to the top floor of the Andrew Johnson Hotel. After hundreds of spectators a day began jamming the elevators, Andrew Johnson management had to evict its most popular tenant.

Construction workers put the finishing touches on Norris Dam, a Tennessee Valley Authority hydroelectric and flood control structure located on the Clinch River. Begun in October 1933, construction on the dam was completed in March 1936. TVA had a significant impact on Knoxville, putting many Knoxvillians to work through tax dollars and bringing hundreds of engineers and technicians to the city.

FROM THE WAR ERA TO RECENT TIMES

(1940–1982)

A Ford dealership located on North Central Avenue.

Knoxville's Federal Building located on Locust Street (ca. 1940).

From its inception in the early 1920s, the idea of creating a national park of the Smoky Mountains region was fraught with seemingly insurmountable financial, cultural, and political issues. By the time President Franklin D. Roosevelt arrived to officially dedicate the park, as seen here on September 2, 1940, more than one million people were visiting each year. Today, the Great Smoky Mountains National Park is the most visited of all the national parks.

Before it ceased operations in 1991, the *Journal* was regarded as the oldest Knoxville newspaper still in circulation. Its first edition rolled off the press in 1885, but the *Journal* claimed its roots traced back to William G. "Parson" Brownlow's controversial *Whig* newspaper, which was founded in Elizabethton in 1838 and moved to Knoxville in 1849. The *Journal* championed state and national Republican causes and was long regarded as the Knoxville *News-Sentinel*'s staunch rival.

This marble gateway monument stands on the corner of Gay and Main in front of the old Knox County Courthouse. It honors Dr. John Mason Boyd, regarded by many as the most famous physician in Knoxville history. Boyd is known for assisting in one of the first successful hysterectomies in medical history and serving as chief of staff at Knoxville General Hospital.

Built in 1909 and opened a year later with an enrollment of 646, Knoxville High School stood at the corner of East Fifth Avenue and Central until the school closed in 1951.

As a vendor offering fresh flowers to passersby, this young fellow leans against his truck on the southeastern corner of the Market House (ca. 1941).

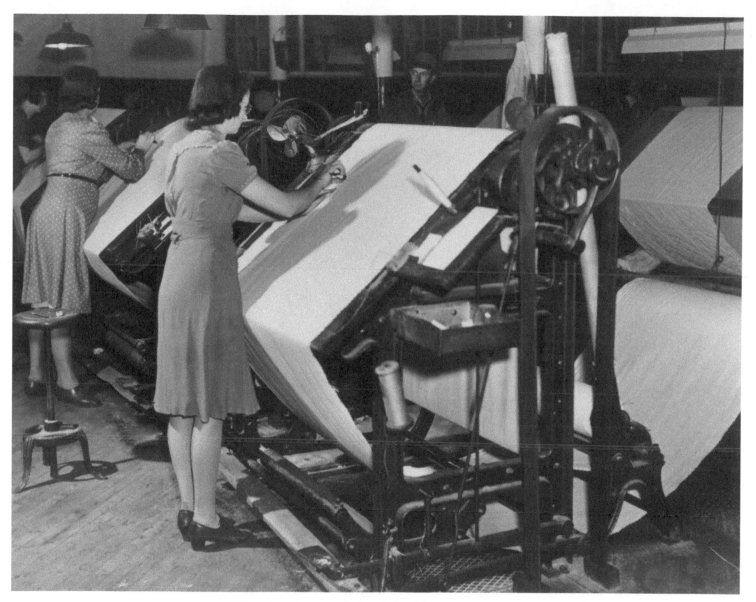

When American men left to defend the nation overseas during World War II, women moved into factory and administrative work, assuming roles in the workforce formerly undertaken by men. While "Rosie the Riveter" was a nationally recognized icon, "Suzie the Sewer" was her counterpart in Knoxville. In this photograph, women employed by Brookside Mills make shelter cloth for Army tents.

As he threw the switch that started the Douglas Dam's generators, steamfitter Patrick P. Marshall said, "I realized that any day I was absent was a day given to the enemy." Marshall, congratulated here by a TVA official, worked 374 consecutive days, from February 1942 to March 1943, to finish construction on the dam, located on the French Broad River.

Young boys aided the war effort during World War II through the Stair Vocational School. The school consisted of high-school age children who enrolled to learn a specific trade such as woodwork, auto mechanics, metalwork, commercial art, and typing. Fred Stair, a former Knox County school board member, established the school in 1934 to provide an opportunity for those students who were not planning to enroll in college to learn a trade (1942).

Women at work in a Knoxville factory during World War II. During the war, more than 14,000 women, 39 percent of the total workforce, were employed in wartime manufacturing plants.

The scene outside the Tennessee Theatre for the premiere of "Invasion Quartet," a British comedy that poked fun at the Nazis who were portrayed as bumbling buffoons.

These cooks prepare dinner in an upscale Knoxville restaurant. For most African-American families living in Knoxville, good jobs were hard to come by. Therefore, both husbands and wives worked to provide for their families.

Big Ridge Lake, which spans nearly 45 acres about twenty-five miles northeast of Knoxville, has been a popular recreational resort since it first opened in May 1934. The lake, along with nearby Norris Park and Norris Dam, was developed by the National Park Service and the Civilian Conservation Corps in cooperation with the Tennessee Valley Authority as one of President Franklin Roosevelt's New Deal programs, which were an attempt to stimulate the nation's depression-era economy using tax dollars.

Knoxville began experimenting with buses in 1928 as the rising popularity and accessibility of automobiles, the stock market crash of 1929, and the Great Depression rendered streetcars nearly obsolete. City officials began requesting that Knoxville Transit Lines convert to buses in the late 1930s; however, the start of World War II disrupted their plans. With the war over in August 1945, the city again requested an all-bus transit system, which was accomplished two years later.

These women select their lunch as they proceed through a cafeteria line.

On August 1, 1947, crowds gathered downtown to witness "the last run" of the electric streetcar as Knoxville adopted an all-bus transit system. The electric streetcar, which first began operating in Knoxville in 1890, reached its height in the 1920s as it fostered the development of suburbs and carried nearly 20 million passengers a year. Knoxvillians pose in front of one of the 12 cars that took part in the solemn procession down Gay Street.

A family of three watches from the comfort of their automobile as three bears approach their vehicle in the Great Smoky Mountains National Park.

A ferry transports passengers and automobiles (ca. 1950).

Once the backbone of Knoxville's economy, manufacturing industries declined after World War II, a significant factor in the city's postwar downturn. In this amusing photograph taken in a local warehouse, a young woman seems to be lifting a pipe over her head, observed by another employee operating a forklift.

The University of Tennessee's famed football stadium has undergone numerous expansions and a few name changes throughout its history. Originally named Wait Field and later Shields-Watkins Field, the university's trustees voted in 1962 to rename the structure Neyland Stadium in honor of legendary coach Robert Neyland. In 21 seasons at UT, Neyland won 173 out of 216 games, five SEC championships, and one national title, defeating Maryland 28–13 in the 1952 Sugar Bowl.

From a seating capacity of 3,200 in 1921 to more than 107,200 today, Neyland Stadium has continued to expand as the success of the University of Tennessee's football program continues to attract fans to "Big Orange Country." This 1950s aerial view captures the ever-expanding stadium when it contained space for nearly 50 thousand spectators.

In an effort to preserve the vitality of the central business district, the Downtown Knoxville Association undertook the construction of the Promenade, which opened in 1955. The Promenade was a city mall that featured convenient parking, covered walkways, and access to stores along Gay Street. Numerous run-down structures located to the rear of the stores on Gay between Union and Wall were demolished to create ample space to build the Promenade and a parking lot.

These young schoolchildren gather around to wash their hands.

Aerial view of downtown Knoxville (1955).

Baptist Hospital of East Tennessee sits on the southern banks of the Tennessee River directly opposite downtown Knoxville. Built in 1948, Baptist Hospital is the flagship hospital of the Baptist Health System and is a premier facility for the treatment of heart, cancer, eye, senior, and women's health.

Knoxville's earliest pilots used various fields to store and operate their planes. In 1929, the city purchased an airport owned by Walter Self along Sutherland Avenue, with the help of Betty McGhee Tyson whose donation of additional land came with the promise that Knoxville's airport would forever be named "McGhee-Tyson" in honor of her son, Charles McGhee Tyson, who died in World War I when his plane went down in the North Sea (1954).

As passenger service arrived in Knoxville, the city's small airport located along Sutherland Avenue could neither support the growing traffic nor the bigger commercial aircraft. In 1935, city officials purchased a tract of land in nearby Alcoa and began construction on a larger airport. On October 15, 1937, the new $726,000 Tyson-McGhee municipal airport, which was completed with Works Progress Administration labor, began operation.

This 1956 aerial view of downtown Knoxville is taken from the south side of the Tennessee River.

For more than 100 years the Market House stood as the economic center where Knoxville's vendors, farmers, and ranchers sold their goods. After a 1960 fire, started accidentally by a ten-year-old boy with a cigarette, destroyed the Market House, the area was cleared as shown in this photograph. Soon thereafter, the Knoxville Downtown Associated put forth plans to design a mall on the site to entice consumers back to downtown.

A woman and little girl walk along Knoxville's downtown business district.

Square dancers perform for an audience assembled on the Mall in Knoxville (1962).

Tom Boerwinkle fights for a rebound in the paint in Knoxville as the University of Tennessee plays the University of Kentucky, their SEC rival and seven-time NCAA champions.

The official in the flagstand on the left waves the flag to start the runabout class of speedboats at the National Outboard Races on Fort Loudoun Lake.

Looking north at the Gay Street Bridge and downtown Knoxville. Both the Andrew Johnson and the Hamilton Bank buildings tower over the skyline.

Construction on the Sunsphere is under way in 1981. As the most recognizable landmark in Knoxville, the 266-foot steel tower was designed to embody the theme of the 1982 World's Fair, "Energy Turns the World." The fair drew around 11 million visitors to the city.

Notes on the Photographs

These notes, listed by page number, attempt to include all aspects known of the photographs. Each of the photographs is identified by the page number, a title or description, photographer and collection, archive, and call or box number when applicable. Although every attempt was made to collect all data, in some cases complete data may have been unavailable due to the age and condition of some of the photographs and records.